Walking
with Our Children:
The Parent
as Companion
and Guide

Essays by **Nancy Blanning**

WECAN
WALDORF EARLY CHILDHOOD
ASSOCIATION OF NORTH AMERICA

Walking with Our Children:
The Parent as Companion and Guide

ISBN: 978-1-936849-39-0

Author: Nancy Blanning
Publications Coordinator: Donna Lee Miele
Copy Editor: Bill Day
Graphic Design, Cover Art and Illustrations:
Sheila Harrington, Studio Five

All articles previously published in LILIPOH from 2010-2017.

Published in the United States by
The Waldorf Early Childhood Association of North America
285 Hungry Hollow Road
Spring Valley, NY 10977
www.waldorfearlychildhood.org

Visit our online store at store.waldorfearlychildhood.org

This publication is made possible through a grant
from the Waldorf Curriculum Fund.

Table of Contents

Guiding Childhood's Inner Life

Quality Time
with Young Children

Allowing Time
to Ripen

*I*f we are lucky enough to have a fruit tree in our back yard, it is such a thrill when it bursts into blossom. We hope a spring snow storm or late freeze will not damage the tiny star flowers. We are grateful when the spent petals fall away because their task of drawing bees is done. Soon the little fruit buds reveal themselves upon the branches. We watch the small, green nubs emerge that will mature into an apple or a peach. If a pesky, hungry squirrel comes near the tree, he is chased away. Or maybe we even put a protective net over the crown of the tree to keep away the birds or other critters that might prematurely peck and damage the bounty we anticipate. As the summer passes, the sour-looking green matures to a warm blush of rose. We would not dream of picking the fruit too soon before it has reached its full ripeness. At last, after all this patient waiting, we harvest what earth, plant, sun, wind, water, and time have provided to us. We revel in the sweetness of the fruit and are grateful.

It is so odd that our society can recognize the rightness of allowing nature time to take its course in our garden but forget how this wise view applies to little children. All developing entities need care and tending and sufficient time to grow. Yet everyone is in such a rush.

When we look at the developmental steps and stages of the child, we see a dependable and lawful order through which the being of the child unfolds. First she gains control of head, then trunk, arms and hands. The chattery movement of the legs finds control and intention to carry her along, with hands, to crawl along the floor. To upright stance she rises, and in time the first tottering steps gain security. Words begin to flow, preparing the foundation for thought. And the child needs to play, to explore, to wonder, to stand in awe at the world she has entered. We hope she will find it so inviting and engaging that she cannot suppress her joy at having entered into life.

This is the child moving from tiny star-flower blossom to ripened fruit before beginning her entry into the world of thinking and learning. She needs to be protected from the pesky squirrels with their nervous nitterings—facts and early academics—and birds which might peck away at her—stabs of sensory overwhelm that shock and bruise. The parents, teachers, and other caring adults stand as the child's sun, radiating warmth and encouragement to grow into her proper ripeness.

The physical sun in the sky shines day after.day and never hurries. It does not worry that the apple is not growing fast enough. It allows time for rightful process to unfold.

Of all the gifts we bestow upon our children, may this be one—allow them time. 🌿

Stories–
Parents' Best Friends

*E*veryone loves stories. As adults we seek out stories in novels and films for many reasons. Stories can carry us off to faraway, alluring times and places. Stories can be just for fun and entertainment. They give us rest from busy schedules and responsibilities and offer a chance to re-create our energies and enthusiasms for life. Stories of other peoples' lives, both real and imagined, can also assist us in exploring life experiences that may pose challenges for us. We can explore through others' feelings and actions how we might approach something similar ourselves, using the story as a mirror to see if its events illuminate our own situation.

Children love stories more than any other age group. Their stage of consciousness is very open to story imaginations. Children instantly flow into the images and pictures stories offer, especially if the story holds some universal images with which their being intuitively resonates. If we think of classic tales like "The Three Little Pigs," "Goldilocks and the Three Bears," and "Little Red Cap," we can recall a child saying, "Tell it again." Something within the child calls for repetition of the images and events in the story. Something the child is experiencing on an unconscious level is being spoken to, which the story helps to explain. For example, we can look to the story of "The Three Little Pigs" as a reflection of the child's experience of "building" and "moving into" the physical house he or she is forming and maturing during the first seven years of life.[1]

Telling stories to our children can also be a parent's a best friend. Teachers in Waldorf schools have long embraced and daily used this insight. Through stories, feelings within the child can be evoked, in a non-scolding, non-moralizing way, that encourage the child to more positive interaction with the world and other people in it. Children live imaginatively in pictures more than thoughts. They are much more open to receiving direction in this way than through logical instruction or (the worst of all) a lecture. With a bit

---

1   *Insight shared by Laurie Clark, Waldorf Kindergarten teacher and teacher educator, summer, 2012.*

of courage to begin and a little practice, this new avenue of interacting more positively with one's own child opens up.

A good friend in our classroom was Bessy Bossy Boots (or he could be Billy Bluster), a story character. Bessy always wanted the biggest and best, and she wanted it quickly. One Halloween the children were going to the farm to choose a pumpkin for carving. Each child had to carry the pumpkin away herself. Bessy raced to the biggest pumpkin and claimed it for her own. No six children could have carried it, but Bessy insisted until she found herself alone, unable to move the gigantic pumpkin. Though she felt very grumpy that she could not have what she wanted, she knew that she did truly want some pumpkin for her jack-o'-lantern. As she looked around, she saw a pumpkin that would fit into her arms and was the perfect shape. The pumpkin had no face yet, but it seemed to Bessy that it winked at her! This was the pumpkin for her.

All a story needs is a character who can indirectly mirror the child's situation, which the story objectively describes without implying any judgment. The result speaks for itself. We can learn about storytelling from experts. Checking with other resources can be a help. But what gives these stories their power is the parent's effort to create the story him- or herself out of love for the child. ✿

Relaxing Time–
Letting Go of Expectations

recent visit to the Waldorf forest kindergarten in Saratoga Springs, New York resonates in memory in a special way. The children whose parents have chosen this program have a consciously simplified environment freed of the temptations and distractions of the busier city life not far down the road. The group spends nearly the whole morning out in nature—no matter the weather—except perhaps for the first hour of morning in deepest winter when the air needs an hour to warm above super-frigid temperatures. Children are called upon to develop heartiness and resiliency in meeting the weather, terrain, practical tasks, and social experiences from which our society too often excessively shelters children. These are all important things for us to appreciate in how these experiences benefit the children's development physically, emotionally, and socially. But we can take these points up at another time because it is something else that stands out in memory from this visit.

A three-year-old girl who was new to the program latched on to my hand as the children began the walk along a trail into the woods. The pathway was made of rounded stepping stones; narrow, slightly-elevated boards to give us walking space above the soggy ground below; similar little "bridges" of two parallel boards that would bounce and spring slightly as we walked their length, challenging our balance; uneven ground that could not be avoided; and puddles that just had to be stepped in. We walked along slowly, three-year old legs having a short stride and some insecurity on the tippy rocks. She held my hand for balance until the path became too narrow and we had to walk single file. Then she went on independently. We set no speed records. And no-one minded. The thirty-two children and five adults walked along in little clusters, some faster, some slower. No one hurried the children along. Getting to our destination took as long as it needed. The littlest children were in no way made to feel inadequate or deficient because they could not walk fast or if a foot slipped on a wet rock and muddy water-proof overalls resulted. Each child was respected for the capacities she had

developed so far, knowing that new skills, competence, and confidence grow upon consolidation of what comes before.

But this still is not really the point. What speaks so strongly in memory is that the teachers allowed the children *as much time as was needed* to walk our little journey. Each child was allowed to do as much independently as she could, no matter how long it took. Expectations were released of how much or how fast things should happen. The day expected less accomplishment because it was so satisfying to complete a few things well.

The little girl moved on to join other children and did not seek my companionship again. She did not need it. She had literally found her feet and her standing with the other children. She had been granted the time to experience what she could accomplish on her own.

We want our children to become confident, independent doers and directors of their own lives. They can, but we adults have to give them the time to find their own strength. We do not need to speed them up. We need to slow ourselves down and let them lead us. We will all benefit.

Transitions—
Helping Children Move through Time

Shifting from one activity to another can be hard work, especially for young children who have no sense of time. When adults announce, "Soon we will . . ." that probably only means to a child: "Not yet." Learning how to transition from one activity to another— waking and readying for the day, leaving for school, meal times, bathing, closing the day and going to sleep—are all pivotal moments. How harmoniously we guide ourselves and our children through these portals of time is important for our quality of life. Times when children are surprised—even shocked—rushed, and especially tired can be the meltdown moments. How can we smooth the way so our children can learn to move gracefully through these passage points?

Hearing extremely busy parents of young children in extremely busy New York City gave me a shocking cultural reference check recently and opened my eyes to something very simple yet profound about transitions. One couple was describing how their three-year-old daughter would not come to dinner. When called to leave her play, she would say, "Five more minutes!" meaning, "No." Then the mother went on to describe how this evening had been particularly busy so they had ordered out for dinner. The signal that dinner was ready was literally hearing the apartment buzzer ring, announcing that the deli was delivering. Food was placed on the table and they ate, after cajoling and then physically transporting their uninterested child to the table. Tummies got adequately filled, but an enjoyable meal it was not.

Please do not take this as indictment of anyone's life style. It is not. It is acknowledgment that our lives are so different, depending on where we live and our cultural milieu. We have enormous diversity to consider in how we creatively respond to life's practical questions with our children, transitions being case in point here.

Children—like human beings of any age—tend to do best when they get signals that a shift in activity is coming. There are common, subtle cues that we may have not thought about, with meal time for example. Usually about an hour before the meal, activity begins in the kitchen. Sounds change—clacking of pans, followed by cooking smells. Children who are old enough are called to do their little chores in scrubbing carrots for the salad, setting the table, arranging a small natural item—flower, stone, shell, or crystal—and candle in the middle of the table. A quiet warning by little rhyme or song announces that toys will rest. Here a parent quietly begins to help the toys go to rest in a slow, deliberate manner. Then the child is quietly taken by the hand and led to the table. As with any scenario, the adults have to practice this over and over again as much as the child.

Busy lives and busy places do not have all these signals. But every family has some. Observe what you do *consistently* and build upon those things. Decide what you can realistically add in to your routine to make the transition time a doorway, not a screeching dash to the next thing. We can always thoughtfully and slowly prepare the table no matter how the food comes. Anticipate in yourself what is coming and prepare the space for your child to walk into it. What we can offer our young children in the early years in navigating transitions lays the foundation for trust that we can manage whatever life brings at other thresholds, too. 🌿

Discipline–
Guiding Angel-Style

iscipline is a hard topic to wrap our minds around in our current times. Many of us remember a time when "right was right and wrong was wrong and children did what their parents and teachers said!" Many more remember a time of questioning this approach and rejecting what seemed to be unfairly authoritarian and rigid. The opposite pole of "anything goes" has its own disappointing complications. Depending upon our philosophical, social or ethical orientations, we see these two polarities at ends of a wide spectrum leaning either toward authoritarianism (with constricting, inflexible attitudes and practices) or permissiveness (where standards shift, change, and bobble around). And our dear children are left standing in confusion and perplexity in the midst of our adult convictions or insecurities about what we actually do think.

"Discipline" has become associated and confused with punishment— "Do as I say or else!" Yet this term actually comes from the word "disciple," which in simplest definition means "pupil" or "learner." While "discipline" can have a stern connotation, one of the foremost definitions from Webster's Dictionary is: "a training that develops self-control and character." Implicit in this definition is that a pupil must have teachers or guides. For the young child the teachers are parents, extended family, and early childhood teachers. Little children have come to earth to learn how to live life. They are looking for guides and companions to help them find their way rightly into the world. They are truly tender little beings like the children lost in the woods of a fairy tale. They are not cerebral and logical. They will be later, but now they follow adult models and directions in image form. To quote Waldorf colleague Steve Spitalny, little children "are just getting started" and are looking to the adults around them to show them the right way into life. Like it or not, that is us. No matter how uncertain we may feel at times, we know more than they do and have to help them step by step.

In my years in the Waldorf kindergarten, the children taught me more than I ever brought to them. One lesson was that confronting a child directly in a stern way, insisting that he or she look me in the eye, rarely—actually never—worked. This was an immediate relationship breaker. The child felt shamed, shut down, and (rightly) shut me out. Discipleship and leadership are based upon trust and warmth. This approach was stern and cold. As a teacher I have observed that if the same approach has not worked five or six times, it never will. So what else to do?

My teacher came in the form of a little boy. He was lively, talkative, and excitable. He would become so engaged in what was happening near to him that the rest of the world ceased to exist. One could say that he seemed "inattentive." The direct approach and insistent voice had seen total failure. Then some inspiration told me to approach him quietly and gently from the side so that he could see me but not feel confronted, bend down to his ear and speak quietly so only he could hear me. The result was miraculous. He nodded his head because I did not require him to speak and then did what was asked.

This did not work every time, but it did a lot. Our relationship of trust and cooperation grew.

I realized, when I learned the Apocryphal Bible story of Tobias and the angel, that I had been gifted with the "Guiding Angel position." Tobias was a young man who had to go on an arduous journey for his blind father. A trustworthy companion was found to accompany him. Through the help of the companion, Tobias successfully completed the task for his father, brought back healing for his father's blindness, and found the proper wife of his destiny. The companion guided Tobias in what to do gently but clearly, from the side. When the father wanted to give the companion a large reward for his service, he revealed himself to be the Archangel Raphael, the archangel of healing, who required no reward.

Children make mistakes because they just don't know how to do things. They are looking for guides to show them the way with understanding and moral clarity. May we be such companions to our children.

PS—With some adjustments, this approach works with adolescents, too. Some situations call for a frontal meeting, but trying side-by-side first can gift us with surprisingly happy results. ❦

The Parent's Question–
But What about Me?

*P*arenting is one of the most rewarding journeys we can ever embark upon and also one of the hardest. It can be relentless. Protecting our children and meeting their needs takes precedence. So we set aside what we may long to develop for ourselves. We can sustain this for a while with equanimity. But moments will come when we feel like we are being pushed over the edge— too little sleep, the family is all sick, or work pressures and deadlines pile up, for example. At these moments our lives get terribly out of rhythm, and everything feels lopsided and out of balance.

This is an honest description of how we can feel. It *can* be a melancholic lament where we assume the role of resentful victim and indulge our grumpy feelings for a while. Parents, too, are human beings after all; and sometimes we are entitled to a good grump. Yet this is a momentary release that usually doesn't change the general situation. But if we can look at this objectively, we see a problem to be solved. What can we do about it?

We can go to the bookstore and choose from rows and rows of parenting advice books. Most of them offer techniques—some of which are valuable and help give us insight into how we are interacting nonproductively with our children. But more often these suggestions deal with superficial responses that do not get to the heart of our humanness. We, as parents, and our children—no matter what their age, from young and dreamy to adolescent and challenging—long for relationship that is warm and respectful. We all carry within ourselves a conviction that it is possible to reach down into the depths of our being where joyful, positive connectedness lies. We are longing to experience in ourselves and others a deep, rich "something" that lies within us as our greater true self. But how do we open that door?

This "something," this essence, which is greater than our everyday being, has been pictured for ages as an invisible reality that some call the realm of the angels, a realm of spiritual realities. We see messengers and protectors from this world in fairy tales and legends. In "Snow White and Rose Red," the angelic being keeps the girls from stepping off a precipice in the dark; in the legend of

Tobias, the angel serves as his guide and companion on a difficult journey.

We picture these entities around our children. We speak prayers for protection and well-being for our precious ones and also picture that these requests are being received and responded to.

But as we mature, the golden thread of connection thins and may seem to have disappeared in our adult lives. Rudolf Steiner, the founder of Waldorf education, explained that this may feel like a sad loss; but it is necessary. We must find our footing in life through our own initiative and resources if we are to grow and develop beyond childhood. When we choose to find this thread again, we do so out of our own free will. This makes it a *deed* instead of a *given* which can be taken for granted. Now, in our busy lives we might say that we will get to this sometime later, when we are not so consumed with daily responsibilities. If opening a new door were just for our own curiosity and comfort, our motivation might not be too strong. But when we find ourselves close to a small "edge" or a big precipice with our children, we have more courage to take a difficult step because we love our precious ones so much and want them to have a good life. We want to be good parents and good human beings.

Dr. Helmut von Kügelgen, a long-time Waldorf educator in Germany, who is himself now in the spiritual world, gave very helpful advice to teachers and parents for opening ourselves again to this special connection. At the beginning of this article rhythm was mentioned. When we feel close to the edge, we have "lost our rhythm and life feels lopsided and out of balance." Dr. von Kügelgen observes that the way to open this special door is to work with rhythm. He points out that the number seven has a special quality and rhythm. There are seven days in the week. The number of days in a month changes, but never the length of the week. There are seven archangels who rule over eons of time. So working in a rhythm of seven may also connect us to this angelic realm. Dr. von Kügelgen suggests that we can work in units of seven days, seven years, or seven minutes.

Remembering myself as a distraught mother of young children approaching that edge, even seven minutes seems too much of a stretch. So how about seven breaths?

When we get distressed and tense, we usually lose the rhythm in our breathing. We need help to reset ourselves. We need a way to step out of the frustrating situation we find ourselves in. We need to pause—take a mini-rest—and then approach the situation anew. This probably sounds like the old counting to ten. Surely there is a forgotten wisdom standing behind that advice, too. But this practice of restraining and refocusing in the rhythm of seven has a deeper intention to reach into that intuitive, deeper world of our best selves. We might even have a little conversation that we make up in the moment during our in-and-out breaths that asks for the unseen to be interested in us and to help us find our way to one another in love.

There is physiological evidence that the eye needs to work in a rhythmic alternation between seeing and resting in order to keep seeing. The retina contains a light-sensitive substance called rhodopsin that enables seeing in a biochemical reaction. It is activated by light, registers the visual image, and then is used up. The eye will no longer register an image on this spot in the retina again until the eye has blinked. It is this blinking, this resting, which allows the seeing forces to regenerate. In a small way, through resting, the eye becomes capable of seeing again.

When we are in a stuck place where we lose our perspective, we need to withdraw for a rest so we can approach it again with new sensing. Pausing, re-establishing rhythm again through the breath, and working with a number that has archetypal significance through time can do no harm. If benefit comes, it will not be just for our children. We will be helping ourselves to answer our question, "What about me?" because a doorway to richer self-knowledge and insight into other human beings will open as well.

Dr. von Kügelgen was a man of great conviction that spiritual realities are available to our lives. If he were hearing this conversation, it is likely that his eyes would twinkle. And he would be sure that through rhythmic practice of seven somethings, in time we would find a door opening to a wonderful surprise.

This column is offered in gratitude for Dr. von Kügelgen's wisdom and encouragement shared with all the Waldorf community, especially early childhood education, to which he was a special friend. December 2016 marked the one hundredth anniversary of his birth.

Work and Play

Practical Work
in the Kindergarten

While sitting at the computer keyboard to render an article, we adults can appreciate our current technology as a tremendous boon. We can communicate quickly, efficiently, and even clearly if we take the time to compose our thoughts well. Labor-saving devices are true liberators in many ways. The time once required for arduously scrubbing clothes in a tub, for example, is freed for other creative pursuits. It is incredible to experience speaking on the cell phone to a daughter in Europe or with a travel agent in the Philippines while traveling across the Midwest in your car. Our adult world can be grateful for the ease these things bring to our practical lives.

Our children, however, have different needs. They are not interested in saving time or having life convenient. They are looking to the adults in their world to show them how to live a human life. They watch those around them with devotion and then recreate all they see through their own actions. Through this imitation, children have always learned how to move in purposeful ways that integrate their bodies and guide them into human activities that contribute to the world and social life. The bending, stretching, lifting, chopping, cutting, stitching, kneading, and stirring have always been fun to do, felt good in the body, and led to a practical result. The children could begin to experience how what they did made a difference in the world. The satisfaction this renders became the foundation for self-esteem.

What children see adults do now is not so interesting. Actions are more passive and miniaturized, not requiring much body movement. Or, it is hard for a little child to understand the practical intent of jogging around the park or walking on a treadmill. This influence shows up in the children's play. A large wood chip now more often becomes a cell phone rather than a boat or the roof for a fairy house being designed over in a quiet corner. A child gestures to push the button to start the dishwasher as cleanup after a meal. That's rather a leap from the traditional practical household activities of previous generations—cooking, sewing, washing, baking, farming, and cleaning, to name a few—that were the content of daily living.

Practical life is part of every day in the Waldorf kindergarten. We grind flour, knead and bake bread, and chop vegetables for our soup. We stitch and sew, wash and clean, saw and sand wood. There is no intention to be a quaint "little house on the prairie." The goal is to let the children experience purposeful activity with a beginning, middle, and end, with concrete result that benefits themselves and others. For the children's sake, the kindergarten keeps alive this heritage of human work so they can experience where our lives have come from. It is also enormously fun to do.

Social Life
in the Kindergarten

When the first Waldorf school was founded in Germany in 1919, western European political structure, economics, culture, and social fabric were in near collapse in the aftermath of World War I. Emil Molt, manager of the Waldorf-Astoria cigarette factory and student of anthroposophy, approached Rudolf Steiner with a question. Did he have ideas for a different educational form which could cultivate a healthy social life upon which these other structures could be built? Out of this question arose Waldorf education. Anthroposophy provides understanding of the developing human being and the rich curriculum offers nourishment to the thinking, feeling, and will life of the child appropriate to his age and development. From first through eighth grade, the student begins with fairy tales; journeys through stories and fables of earlier times, such as mythologies and ancient civilizations, leading to Greece and Rome, the Middle Ages, and explorations; and ends with the biographical pictures of inspiring individuals from modern history. The students quietly travel through the panorama of how social life has developed through the epochs up to our time. In story and picture, the students see as well how each human being develops from dreamy childhood to standing as a responsible, caring member of society.

Now what is the curriculum of early childhood? There are practical life activities—cooking, cleaning, and making—along with festival celebrations, painting and drawing, stories, songs, and playing. These enjoyable activities help develop capacities of the whole human being. Also embracing the emerging community of children, like the twelve blessing fairies in "Briar Rose," is Waldorf education's commitment to help develop skills for a healthy social life.

Little children come to earth as apprentices who will need guidance and role modeling from the adults around them. They will not know how to use tools and automatically understand the intricacies of a craft. In the craft of social life, too, children are beginners. In the classroom we understand that they will make many social missteps. "Briar Rose" also has a thirteenth fairy that causes havoc. Human beings are not always kind, patient, and generous. We sometimes have intentions and desires that do not harmonize with others around us. We can feel frustrated and thwarted and may lash out with angry, unkind words. Sometimes we even push or hit. The thirteenth fairy insists that we explore the selfish, darker side of ourselves, too, which is also a gift of our birth. Teachers know that these things will happen. When they do, we see it as expression of stepping out of ego-centricity into social life— clumsily, timidly, awkwardly, sometimes forcefully. It takes much practice to learn self-restraint and to appreciate that our friends have wants and needs as valid as our own.

What is "discipline" in the Waldorf kindergarten? It grows first out of creating rhythm and routine that give the children security in knowing the expectations of each day. Productive, useful activities guide hands; stories help to guide feelings. If children get out of their social depth, the teacher is always there to intervene and be the strong boundary when needed.

Our society is hyper-vigilant about bullying, and so should we be. No one should be intimidated or oppressed by deliberately directed ill will. Yet there will always be bumps and thumps within the day, patches of discord. The healthy social life is not constant happiness or absence of challenge. It is where each individual develops strength and flexibility by bumping into one another and again finding equilibrium. The kindergarten is a social rock tumbler. The stones have to grind against each other to polish away imperfections and impurities to reveal the gem-like beauty of what lies concealed within.

Space Exploration–
Adventures in Risk

*S*tories about outer space exploration always draw a good audience. There
is adventure, exploration of the unknown, challenge and danger, insistence
upon confronting obstacles, risk taking, and calls for courage even when
one is afraid. Willingness to take a big risk is always part of the scenario. The
adventurer has to be willing to risk losing something in order to become
victorious at the story's end. Usually in the process, there is an unexpected gift
of self-discovery as well. There is an inner adventure as well as the apparent
outer one. In real life, this has been confirmed by several American astronauts
who describe being mightily changed by their experiences in space. New
perspectives of self and world have grown out of their adventures. We greatly
admire these intrepid explorers for their courage and willingness to be so
daring. We may well hope that our own children will grow up to have such
qualities of strength and determination. So where does this all start and how
can we encourage it?

The first explorer of space is the young child. The child enters the earthly
world as an adventurer in a strange land. He has the task of learning the
contours and geography of his own body first. Learning to know the limbs and
head and trunk and how they all work together is the first task. Then comes
venturing out into the space of his environment—first within the home and
then into the broader world. Little by little, exploration into space extends
further and further from the parents and what is familiar. And normal, healthy
curiosity insists upon asking, How far can I go? How high can I climb? What
will my body do as my "space ship"?

Recently I watched a 4-year-old in a nursery class. When free play
time began, he had a clear mission in mind. He went directly to claim two
beanbag chairs. These he placed precisely about five feet away from a study
ledge. He clambered up onto a sofa, climbed from there on to the ledge,
set his leap, and then sailed through the air in a great arc, landing exactly
on the beanbags. This he did over and over again through the whole play
time. Teachers were carefully monitoring him as he became his own personal

rocket ship. No one interfered with his intention to explore the capacities of his body and the courage to take the risk that his inner "star ship captain" had set as the mission. This was not a robust-looking child. He was rather thin and pale, looking physically fragile. But he did not doubt his capacity to do this feat. His face was transformed by looks of delight and satisfaction with his success. He was exploring outer space and discovering his own inner space filling with confidence and competence. He was learning how far he could extend himself into the world.

This little fellow took a risk. He was lucky that no one prevented him from this exploration out of adult fearfulness that he might get hurt. He was not discouraged from trying because of fear that he would fail. He got to discover his own competence.

We live in a world where fear has a mighty grip. We are reluctant to let our children take risks, to test themselves and discover new lands or limitations through their own efforts. Our desire to protect can become a straitjacket for the growing child if it is held too tightly. It is my hunch that the parents of adventurers held their breath as their children jumped, leapt, and tested the limits of self and space. But they did not interfere. May we adults be courageous in allowing each of our children to take adventurous steps to explore his or her own universe of outer and inner space so they can enter their futures with confidence.

Family Tasks
and Togetherness During Autumn's Transition

Summer, with its glorious out-breath, gives such freedom to explore and enjoy the out-of-doors. There is so much to do: playing in the sunshine, digging in dirt, playing in water, swimming, biking, building forts, exploring, and creating out of whatever is at hand. The bigger the pieces of wood, cloth, or rope, the finer the dress-up possibilities for different characters and adventurers, the better it is. Children can play outside until dusk, so the need for entertainment is small. A bath to wash those summer feet, a story, and off-to-bed make for a relaxed rhythm.

Then autumn comes. Night encroaches earlier each evening until it is dark at 5 o'clock. As the natural world, after its glorious last blast of colored leaves and ripened fruit, begins to fade and whither, so are we beckoned to retreat into our homes. We were vast and expanded and now have to contract into small living spaces, both within our homes and within ourselves. This can feel somber. It can also be problematic. How do we fill the evening hours before bedtime? How do we get the evening chores done with children under our feet and at loose ends? What can we do to avoid the screen-entertainment temptation when the children proclaim, "We don't have anything to do!"

But stories the children hear about Mother Earth and her seed babies give us a clue to what we can do. These tales reassure that all the activity of summer has not ceased; it has just changed location. There is nestling and resting in the sheltering earth, which retains the warmth gifted from the summer sun. Seeds, bugs, and burrowing creatures are working to wait yet prepare for the reawakening in spring. Their activity is intense but quiet and not visible to our eyes. But they are doing their work. Autumn is a time of transition. We can transition into our interior spaces, too, and fill them with activity.

Children love to "do" and they love to work. But they do not like to do it alone. They like to "do" in company with others, particularly their parents. Instead of being entertained, they like to cook and help prepare the evening meal. Depending on the age of the child, that can mean washing a bowl over and over in a wash tub with a little sudsy water while others cut and cook. It can mean peeling a carrot over and over until it is shredded to add to the salad. It can mean the whole family gathering in the living room to sort and fold the laundry. Little ones can pull out socks into a pile and begin to match pairs while clothes that really matter are folded precisely by others. Someone reads a story while others fold or everyone sings a song together. A simple nursery rhyme with little children will do. They love to sing it over and over. Simple, hand-made holiday gifts and cards can be started well in advance and worked on for only 15 or 30 minutes at a time. The trick is to keep the projects and materials simple and limited so no one gets overwhelmed or feels unsuccessful. Half-hour jobs or less—washing the kitchen floor, everyone with a sponge; wiping down a few cabinets at a time; stirring together granola to roast in the oven—can be saved for after school or the evening so the family can do them together.

All summer the natural, elemental world has been working to tend and nurture its space. The sun's warmth has stirred everything into activity. When we direct our activity into our own home and soul spaces, the expansive activity of the summer has condensed into the quieter inner hum of the family. The warmth is generated through everyone being and working together in a shared activity. Children feel their parents' warming interest through the time and patience shared in being escorted into the tasks of life. It does not matter if things take a bit longer or are less perfectly done. Everyone has to practice before we get good at something. And who are better teachers for children than the parents who love them so dearly? Who can feel bereft or discouraged by the darkening of autumn with this warmth and light of interest in one another glowing inside the home? 🍂

Simple Playthings
for Girls and Boys—Encouraging Creativity and Independent Thinking

*I*t is an amusement to adults when a young child opens a gift. The excitement is high when the box is opened. There is fascination to see what is inside. There is usually some animated play, and then the child leaves the toy behind and plays for a long time with the box. The adult thinks, "How silly! The child just doesn't understand what the best part is."

But the little one does understand—so much better than the grownups. The little child is yet living in a sense of fluid creativity and is not attached to things with firm definition. In fact, a toy with its defined limits becomes boring because it does not allow the child's fantasy to change it into different things. A Jack-in-the-box, for example, does the same thing over and over again. After a while there is no more surprise and little possibility to use it in a different way. A box, however, is wide open to the child's exploration. It can be a cave; a turtle shell; a table; a car, train, boat or plane to ride in; a stove for cooking; a baby's bed; a garage to drive the car into; and so on. All of this activity is coming from within the child in an almost endless flow. The ability as an adult to be able to create one's own inner pictures and imagine in such a creative way is highly sought after. Some of the most successful CEOs are individuals who can "think out of the box." Likely they could think "in the box," "around the box," "on top of the box," and hiding "under the box" as children.

But this can be suppressed or side-tracked by an endless parade of cleverly designed entertainment that distracts, even lures, the child away from her own inner activity. This is one reason why the flood of screens and technology toward younger and younger children is so alarming. Everything comes from the outside with no requirement and no opportunity to be active within one's independent being. The images provided by technology also become repetitive, like the detailed toy with limited play options; so there always has to be a new version to buy to keep the child engaged.

Simple, open-ended playthings are what serve the child. A round slice cut from a slender tree trunk can be a plate, the burner on a stove, a wheel to roll on the floor, or a pathway to tiptoe upon. A basket of chestnuts becomes soup for dinner, marbles to race across the floor, treasure to carry in a little sack. Tufts of colored wool may one moment be fried eggs for breakfast, carrots and tomatoes for dinner, fairy fluff, a fire, or even a beard if the adult can supply some sticky tape.

We have continued societal debate as to whether we "genderize" children by giving them stereotypical gender-related toys. Girls given dolls and domestic playthings are thought to assume those roles and miss their chances to become doctors, engineers, or mathematicians. Boys receiving trucks and "aggressive" toys will not develop sensitivity and will become dominating personalities. Simple toys are gender-neutral. What a girl or boy does with a disk of wood comes out of the individual child; nothing external demands that it be utilized in a particular stereotypical way. All is open for the child to be creative, flexible and independent in his or her play. As an added bonus, bits of wood, stones, chestnuts, corn cobs, and sea shells require a bit of collecting and smoothing, perhaps. But they do not cost much. Wonder why commercial America hasn't mentioned this as a play alternative? ⟿

Creative Supplies
for Happy Working Play

*I*f anyone had said that two plastic dish pans, a few unbreakable dishes and cups, soapy water, a dish brush or two, and old towels would provide the best day of working play for our grandchildren, even I would have been skeptical. Waldorf kindergartens are known for their natural materials, lovely toys, and beautiful silks to speak to the child's imagination. I had certainly seen those used to create happy play times and had provided an assortment of them in our home. But the dress-up basket lay untouched, the lovely hand-made dolls remained sleeping in their cradles, and the grandchildren clambered around the kitchen sink. The little ones were hungry for something else. "We want to help, Grandma!" was their cry.

When parents hear this request, they consider how much extra work it will make if the children "help." Wanting to "get things done," the parent often says, "Go play," and then gets on efficiently to finish the task in a tidy way. But there is something addlepated and indulgent within grandparent brains that says, "Sure!"

Now the task was to wash dishes. The kitchen sink was tall and narrow. There was no room for one adult and two children standing on stools to help at the sink. What to do? Plastic dish pans have long been a staple item in the household, endlessly useful for small children to fill, carry, push, sit in, build with, and even stand on. But this day two were gently filled with sudsy water. The opened dishwasher door found a new use. It became the "table" on which the wash pans sat, just the right height for little children and impervious to some extra water. Cups and dishes were washed and scrubbed again and again. Water splashed. Children and the floor got a little wet. It was warm so there was no worry about anyone getting chilled.

The floor got wetter. Small puddles were forming and the children looked up anxiously. So now it was time for the old towels. We started by just putting the towels on the floor to soak up the water. Then we thought to scooch the towels across the puddles with our bare feet. Soon we were towel skating on the floor, and the kitchen tiles were having their turn to be cleaned.

With the addition of an actual mop bucket and a couple of scrubbing brushes as our tools, the floor got a good cleaning. Towels finished up the mopping and were carried, heavy and wet, outside to dry in the sun. Our time ended with a cleaner kitchen; happy, satisfied children; and a grandmother standing in awe at the beauty of how easy all this had been.

The practical ingredients for this lovely time were simple and cost little money. The commercial world would like us to believe that fun can only be had through complicated, flashy, expensive, technologically conceived "toys." It will absolutely drive the toy makers nuts that we take our lead from the children instead of their economically driven attempts to influence and persuade us. Give the children a container, something to put in it, and something to stir and pour the something in the container. The children will supply the imagination to make something miraculous happen.

And there is one other essential. That is for the adults to not worry about mess or efficiency or about getting things done in a non-traditional way. That is for the adults to say "Yes" to the child's implicit question, "Can I try it myself too, please?"

Go Play

My childhood memories often include my mother saying, "Go play." To us that usually meant to go outside, find a neighborhood child or two, and figure out what to do. There were a few essential toys—a doll or two, a truck, a bicycle, roller skates (the metal kind that clamped onto the toes of our substantial Buster Brown shoes), and Mother's high heels or Father's heavy leather shoes for clumpy-walking dress up. There was a spade for digging in the garden and a beloved egg beater to crank around in soapy water and build up mountains—well, maybe what looked like mountains to us children—of suds. Also on hand were a few worn-out bed sheets and an old blanket for building forts by draping these over some discarded two-by-fours which lay alongside the wall of the garage. If the weather was too cold or wet, the building went on inside with sofa cushions and dining room chairs as our construction essentials. By today's standard, this does not seem like much. But this was no deprivation or poverty. These items kept us endlessly busy figuring out different ways to use them. We did not know that we were creating; we were just doing. Materials were simple and the activity was satisfying. And all the while we children were playing, our parents were doing the necessary work of each day.

Fast-forwarding to today, we see many shifts in practice and attitude. Play opportunities for children are often structured around concerns about safety in our increasingly uncertain and unpredictable world. So we have the playdate replacing the more open-ended, free-range "go play" of former times. Finding your own "what to do" is being replaced by toys that entertain, dazzle, or instruct. These toys are often limited in what kind of play they suggest to the child. With their narrowed versatility, these toys offer fleeting satisfaction to the child and are soon abandoned.

The lives of parents have also changed. Working parents have limited awake contact time with their children. They want "quality" interaction with their offspring when possible. Parents who do not work outside the home often have more open time in the day because conveniences have lightened our household work load. These parents are searching for activities to fill the day. So more and more parents are "playing" with their children. This can involve getting down on the floor and playing with the child's toys as though the adult were a child. It can also mean following along behind the child to make sure he or she stays entertained and is constantly reassured of the adult attention and presence.

To interact playfully with our children is essential. Dressing and cradling a baby doll, having a pretend tea party, building a castle in the sandbox, racing trucks across the floor, running, dancing, tickling, and wrestling are wonderful and enjoyable as short interludes. But for the adult to become the child's playmate as a long-term activity can be a kind of slavery for the adult and a handicapping limitation for the child. Why? Isn't it rejecting and neglectful to not respond to the child's request, "Play with me"?

What is play? The answer is different for adults and children. One dictionary definition states that play is "recreation." Adults conceive of recreation as something that gives relief from the effort and stresses of work. We often think of sports and athletics as recreational activity; media entertainment also fills a lot of "down" time. Through playful activities we refresh our vital energies. Adult play can help us relax our attention and escape from the responsibilities of life for a little while.

For children, the process is reversed. Children play to find their way into life, not escape from it. Play for them is an act of creation. Children take the experiences and impressions of the world and re-create them in a form they can manipulate and direct. Through this process, these young ones can imaginatively explore the world and make sense out of it in a way that suits their level of consciousness. It is said that play is a child's work. When viewed as creative activity, we can see that play is serious business. When they play, children focus intensely, concentrating on re-creating what they have witnessed in the world, digesting the experience so it becomes "owned" in their emerging world-construct.

It is important for us to observe and respect children's play process. We can protect the space in which they can unfold this unique capacity of early childhood which we adults have become distanced from. We can give models of purposeful human activity for children to imitate and explore. But when we become playmates, we are trying to imitate being a child—which we are not— and actually get in their way. They do not need us as playmates. They need us as guides into human life. When the environment is right—not narrowed by pre-scripted toys or adult fearfulness—and we say "Go play," we are releasing them to one of the most important creative activities for their present and future.

Supporting
Healthy Development

Movement in Early Childhood
Developmental Magic or Nourishment?

*E*arly childhood is the gateway to healthy development and a sense of comfort and happiness in one's own physical body. Much of this is accomplished through play and the freedom of movement that play invites. Not so long ago when childhood was less structured and allowed freer exploration of the world, this important development happened without our awareness. We saw children actively run, play tag, skip, climb, teeter-totter, balance, and roller skate. We could witness how these children developed full-body coordination and skill in movement. But what we could not see is that integration of the sensory systems also develops through this activity. Neurological development and brain integration essential for the academic and intellectual skills our society so highly values is also forming. Current neurological research confirms that the movements children go through in work and play create important neural pathways and foster brain development. Stated simply, movement builds the brain. The richer in variety and more frequent the movement activities, the better it is for brain development.

Children still do all of the activities described above, but today the mood is different. Fearfulness has invaded the world and a well-intentioned gesture of protectiveness restricts childhood activities even more. Testing balance by scrambling onto rocks, climbing trees, or walking along a fence ridge is discouraged if not prohibited because of fear of injury. When a child goes out to play, instead of wishing, "Have fun," the adult is more likely to say, "Be careful."

Enchantment with media and computers poses additional challenges. These keep the child occupied and safe, we justify; in using computers, children develop cognitive intelligence by using educational programs, we continue. Leaving aside the wider questions about how media use negatively affects children, every passive moment children spend in front of a screen robs them of the opportunity to move and build themselves physically and neurologically for their own futures.

Playful, exploration-filled movement is a critical heritage Waldorf early childhood education stands to guard and encourage. This happens daily in Waldorf programs. Abundant free play time, both indoors and out, invites children to move according to their own imaginative scripts and explore their environments and fine tune the movement and coordination of their own bodies. Lively imaginations in daily circle time, obstacle courses, movement adventures, and traditional ring games guide the children into the healthy movements their development craves.

Our own home hours with our children are also critically important. Dance classes, sports, gymnastics, etc. entice us into thinking that they will satisfy this need for movement experience. Yet these generally have a "right" or "wrong" way to move. This can demoralize a young child who is just learning to direct body movement. Moving in directed, prescribed ways also limits freedom to explore every nook and cranny of muscles and bones, balance and posture, that help us find our stance in the world. Every chance to run, leap, balance, swing, twirl, lift, skate, slide, roll, start-stop, and then rest is an invitation to a healthy future.

Touch, Warmth
and Boundaries

The word "boundaries" comes up often in common parlance these days. Someone has "crossed a boundary" inappropriately. Parents and teachers may lament that a child has "no sense of boundary." We may feel a personal need to "establish a boundary" in professional, social, or family life. Other expressions that imply boundary are in saying, "I need my space," or someone else is "in my space." These all describe having both a visible physical space and experiencing what is intrusion into invisible social and psychological space around us as well. It is healthy for us to recognize boundaries. Then we can be respectful in holding appropriate distance, meeting harmoniously at a boundary line, and crossing a boundary with sensitivity when necessary. How does this experience and knowledge of boundary come about?

Interestingly enough, Rudolf Steiner explained that it begins with the sense of touch. We usually think that with touch we reach out and gain information about the world outside of ourselves. This is true. But Steiner emphasized that the more essential service of touch is to give experience of personal, physical boundary. When I reach out and touch something, I experience where I end and where the rest of the world begins.

At birth the touch sensors in the skin are awake and active. But the sense of touch in the wider context needs education to establish a sense of boundary to the outside world and nurture an experience of wholeness on the inside, that the child's body is an integrated whole. Fussy babies calm down when they are swaddled. This gives confirmation of being securely held in the body and not lost in the space of the world.

Touch is further educated and matured by the materials that come into contact with the skin. Are clothes comfortable natural fiber and reassuring to the body contour, or are they scratchy and ill-fitting? Does clothing invite pleasant living inside the boundaries of the physical body, or is it too constricting or too loose? Constriction may lead to disregarding boundaries and blasting out through them. Insufficient experience of boundary may lead to being ravenous for touch, intruding into others' space to find one's own containment.

We experience warmth primarily through the skin. While not the same as touch, warmth (or its absence) affects the quality of touch. When we are physically warm and feel the body comfortably embraced though touch experiences, we can relax and be content to stay within our own physical boundaries.

Rudolf Steiner said that touch, along with balance and self-movement, lays the foundation for how we will be able to reach into the social world. We "touch" other people through our gaze, tone of voice, and warmth of heart as well as with our physical hands. If a child's developing sense of touch has been nourished and tended with warmth and care, his own sense of boundary has a good chance of feeling comfortable and safe. He will be able to perceive and respect the boundaries of others because he feels secure within himself. This confidence can then radiate out as respect for the boundary lines of others.

What a provocative thought it is to consider that educating and caring for a sense we take for granted—touch—is also laying the foundations for healthy social life.

Technology
and Young Children

Airports are good places to see the explosion in use of technology by all age groups. Adults and teenagers are on laptop computers and iPhones. Kids in general with increasing numbers of younger and younger children are plugged into an "iSomething" to keep them quiet and focused on a screen. We justify this media use because it keeps children from moving around and disturbing us. The children may even be seeing something "educational" on the screen. And we marvel at how savvy and skilled the children are becoming at using these electronic devices, thinking that this is giving them a head start in life.

If we look deeply at what motivates our choices here, we may also see fear lurking. We fear that our boisterous children might disturb others, fear that the little ones will not learn enough fast enough to be successful in life, fear that our children will not be competitive in a technological society if they do not begin use at an early age. There is an unspoken attitude in society that if a child does not show advanced skills at a precocious age, he or she is already behind. So the general attitude pushes academic and technological expectations on younger children with increasing intensity. Time is dedicated—often by using screens—to win this race. Childhood as a delicate time to explore the world in its fullness gets shortened.

Interestingly, both the technology argument and Waldorf early education agree upon an important point. The years of early childhood, from birth to seven years, are deeply important and should not be misused. But the debate is over how this time is best utilized to serve the child's most broad development. Waldorf early childhood education has always affirmed that during these early years the foundation for future capacities, abilities, and skills are formed; and active engagement in the world is the best way to strengthen these.

Modern neurology looks to brain research to watch how this development happens. Research confirms two things. Parts of the brain that are used repetitively develop most. Parts that are unused wither away;

whatever potential that may have rested in unused pathways is sloughed off. Greater diversity of activity develops more parts of the brain, a more "enriched brain." MRIs show that movement of all sorts, engagement of all the senses, speaking, singing, interacting socially, and so on, stimulate activity across the entire brain.

Interacting with a screen has limitations. Screen time engages the child's eyes, ears, and finger tips to respond to predetermined right or wrong responses. The brain is developing connections between these areas. The rest of the child's body—and brain—is essentially passive.

We also know that screen use is not limited to airports but occupies other parts of our children's days. Time spent in front of screens takes away from active play and exploration that has previously filled children's early years. Children who have developed lots of "brain potential" in the early years are equipped to meet the challenges of the future. Let us put our fears aside and let the children play with the world and with each other. Research shows that this develops an adaptable and versatile brain for learning potential and problem solving. Screen time can wait.

Overload:
Over-Stimulated and Under-Protected

*I*nformation, useful and trivial, wanted or not, bombards us constantly. Our senses are continually stimulated. In self-protection, I have personally found an email access that avoids a "home page" that assaults me with the latest celebrity news, disaster of the moment—whether actual or threatened—and lots of ads to tell me what I need to buy for a happy life. These things I can choose to consider if and when I want to. My freedom as an adult lets me have this choice.

But for little children it is quite different. Rudolf Steiner, the founder of Waldorf education, observed that the young child is a "total sense organ." To understand this, we can think of our own eyes. When they are open, we see everything that is before us whether we want to or not. As we grow older, we can choose whether or not to pay attention to what we see; but the visual impression registers in the eye no matter what. The eye cannot select what it sees.

This is what little children are like. They cannot select what they "see" with all of their senses. Here we mean not only sight, but also hearing, touch, taste, and smell, for example. Everything that comes toward the child goes in and makes an impression. If we think of our own adult experience of information and sensory overload, what must it be like for a little child who is quite defenseless? Some children know that they are overwhelmed and shrink away from contact with the world; they find their protection in retreat. Others just begin to "short out." Their nervous systems become so stressed that no more can be tolerated. Little explosions, meltdowns, and otherwise wacky behavior send the children—and us—into tailspins.

There is an attitude in our society that everyone has to experience and learn things as fast as possible, the earlier the better. Otherwise our children are at risk of being "left behind." So little children are expected to accomplish sophisticated learning and information assimilation at earlier and earlier ages. Somehow it is believed that cognitive development can be accelerated by giving more and more information faster and faster. And so the societal expectations push us along.

Yet if we look at the child in other areas of development, we see a very different picture. We know that babies need lots of sleep. We do not decide to keep them awake so they can learn about the world faster. Our good sense lets the baby literally sleep his way into life to start with, only gradually becoming more and more wakeful. We know that their digestion develops gradually. We do not feed steak and oysters to an infant. We give them foods that are easy to digest, only adding in new tastes and smells step-by-step as their system matures. We observe that the children do best when life in this way is slower paced.

So it is with sensory stimulation and information. Since children cannot shield themselves from overload, the caring adults around them need to be their filters. The facts we need to know about the world we gather in time. What the Internet and other media share is not carefully selected to encourage healthy development. Fewer visual images; less noise; quiet, meaningful speech; and purposeful life activities introduce the world more slowly but surely. The little child can step toward life and greet its experiences a little bit at a time. To greet the world in this way is a relief for children. They can prepare to meet the complexities and details of life with interest and strength when they are older and stronger. "Overload" is for the adults to deal with, not our new, little people. ✿

Preventing Addiction

*T*his may seem a strange topic when we are talking about early childhood. But it is in the earliest years of life that addiction prevention forms its bedrock. To understand this, we need to picture the pathway of human development to see where addiction prevention begins. This is an important journey to take to see what helps and what dangers lie ahead for our precious, young children.

Addiction prevention begins when the child is very young. This realization was startlingly emphasized at an international Waldorf educators' conference in Dornach, Switzerland in spring, 2015. Teachers from all levels of Waldorf education—early childhood, grades, high school—and physicians gathered to understand and discuss how to support critical moments of development in our children's lives. The once typical landscape of childhood has changed with the world's fast pace, use of technology, fearfulness, and general sense of uncertainty and insecurity that surround our lives. That children will achieve healthy development in our modern world is not at all a given anymore.

Of all these changes, the one that is most intrusive into daily life is the use of screens. It is common to see very little children with screens in hand, totally still and absorbed in whatever they see in this tiny, virtual world. The child's first seven years is the essential time to develop a sense of inner strength, initiative, confidence, and competence that can protect them when facing the challenges of the future. Adults consider screens to be useful tools. They can be fascinating, even alluring. But this media use with young children can whisper them away from developing strong and independent self-hood.

Screen use is a crucial question we must consider for our children. It is subtle to consider, but exposure to screens can play a part of this picture of addiction. This is a bold and challenging statement, no doubt offensive to some. But please read on. The following picture of child development will describe where pitfalls await but also where possibilities to support a healthy sense of self and resilience lie.

A first question addressed at the educators' conference was, "What is addiction?" Dr. Bettina Lohn, school doctor for Waldorf students in grades 8-12 in Switzerland, defines addiction as dependency upon a substance or a behavior. There develops a compulsion for an external experience in order to "feel good." A surprising statistic indicates that addictions to substances— alcohol, tobacco, coffee, chocolate, marijuana—are not increasing. But behavior addictions—such as gaming, internet media use, video games, shopping, self-injuring, cutting, and anorexia—are all on the rise. Participation in some of these activities is common in moderation in ordinary life. But a threshold has been passed when the consumption or behavior becomes a compulsion. It is hard to discern where addiction actually starts. But once established, there can be enormous consequences to health, finances, personal development, emotional and psychological well-being, and social relationships.

To "prevent" means to do something to keep the addiction from happening. We have substance abuse education programs in schools to inform children of the dangers of experimentation with different substances. We know that young people, particularly adolescents, have not developed the discernment or maturity in neurological development to make sensible decisions. They tend to be risk takers and feel invulnerable. Many young people experiment with substances or risky behaviors, but only a few develop addictions. Why? What makes the critical difference that allows some to "taste," then say "No, thanks," and move on?

We want to protect our children from harmful influences. These education programs are important, but something more has to have come much, much earlier as a general prevention for every child. Warning and moralizing about the dangers of addictions will have little effect if the foundation of inner strength has not been supported very early in life. We must consciously encourage and allow our children to strengthen themselves.

Here is where we touch upon the nature of early childhood. When we think about young children, we see that they are *doers*. They want to *do* everything, sometimes to our frustration and chagrin. The child has a natural drive to explore and discover the world. In doing so, the child begins to develop his or her own experience of individual competence. To push and pull, take apart and put back together, to dig and fill, to lift and carry, to dump and pick up, to twirl and spin, to climb and jump, to fall and stand again are things children repeat over and over until they feel competent. This is one way that they develop confidence and learn to "feel at home" in their physical bodies. To feel confident and trust that the body will do what the child intends allows her to "feel good" as a result of her own actions. No outside substance or distraction is necessary. The child has strengthened her own will and sense of competence through doing. Being active in the world rather than passively receiving or timidly holding back is a first step in preventing vulnerability to addiction.

All children have a natural drive to find their own independence. This is a gradual process that needs approval and support from the caring adults around them. To begin with, little children are at the mercy of their environment. They have no discrimination. All is interesting and equal to their experience. They cannot discern what is good or bad, and they imitate what they see around them. We adults have to play that discriminating role in their lives so this inner, independent self-longing to grow is not "hijacked." Screens may make life seem easier by engaging a child's attention to keep him quiet. But screen time is a will-breaker. It supplants the independent self that is longing so deeply to establish itself in this earthly life with something artificial, something "in place of self."

The first seven years of life particularly is the time for the will to develop. We speak about will power, which needs to develop in two directions. One direction is in having the will power to restrain, to hold back, to "just say no." The other direction is having the will to *do*, to have initiative and follow through, even if the task is not inherently fun or interesting. To resist is an act of will that is born out of the will to do. *With screens, the only real act of will is to turn it off.* If the satisfaction realized through one's own activity has been experienced enough, the lure of "feeling good" through some external means holds less temptation.

All human beings seek confirmation that we have a meaningful place in the world. We want to know that it matters that we are alive on this earth and that the things we do contribute. Many people who develop addictions do not believe their lives have meaning. They turn to substances or compulsive behaviors to distract themselves from the feelings of meaninglessness. In addition to our parental care and nurturing love, we show our children that they matter by giving them meaningful work to do that contributes to our social welfare. To engage our children in the work of the home is an act of addiction prevention. Small chores to begin with—silverware on the dinner table, carrying one's plate to the sink, washing dishes by hand, folding napkins, sweeping with whisk broom and dustpan, and so on—cause the young child to develop habits that strengthen selfhood.

Children want to be self-sufficient, so they need the opportunity to develop self-care skills. Allowing them to do this takes lots of time. In our fast-paced, busy lives, this is hard. But making the time in these early years to struggle into snow pants and boots enough times to figure it out is a step toward addiction prevention. A three-year-old girl proved this strongly. She struggled and struggled to take off her snow wear, hang her sweater on a high hook, and put on her indoor shoes. It took time, but it was the most important thing happening in the world for her at that moment. When she had succeeded, she turned with a smile and said, "I do it myself." Being both challenged and *allowed* from early childhood onward to "do it myself" strengthens the child against the lure of seeking this satisfaction from something external in the future.

Young children are naturally imitative. They mirror back whatever they see others do. If what they see is purposeful, this is what they will reflect back to us. If they experience what looks to them like passivity, doing nothing, they will imitate this too. Children are hard pressed when they mostly see adults speaking and texting on cell phones or working on computers. If children do not see steps of preparation in cooking a meal, shoveling snow with shovels, clearing leaves with rakes by hand instead of using leaf blowers, mending something that is broken, or stitching up a torn piece of clothing, they have few examples of meaningful things to do. Watching people use technology has no content or result in practical life to the children's perception. Children are longing for what is real and purposeful, not for what is virtual. To help our children strengthen here, we must give them examples of real activity where something is accomplished through human effort. This means that we have to shovel the snow ourselves with the children at our side with their own shovels, and so on. We may have to come out of our technological, convenient lifestyle habits to go out of our way to give children these experiences. Yet anything that will help our children toward a healthy future and strength in personhood is a huge investment and a small sacrifice in the long term.

Modern technology has relieved us of much arduous work that kept earlier generations busy from dawn to dusk. This has liberated time and energy to explore opportunities to develop our humanity in fuller and richer ways. We have leisure time. How will we use it? Media producers of all sorts are waiting to fill that void for us with videos, electronic games, educational programs, and films. The things we see on screens are alluring, fascinating, exciting—and addicting. As described above, early childhood especially is the time for activity, for developing one's own will forces to purposefully *do* and experience one's effectiveness in the world. It is the time for reaching out into the world to explore. It is the time for seeing and imitating purposeful activity as a template for acting purposefully in the future. It is the time for strengthening self-initiative.

When our children sit in front of a screen, they are not reaching out into the world through their own initiative and activity. They are being *pulled into* a world created by someone else's intention. They are not moving; they are not exploring and creating their own experiences of the natural world. They are not strengthening their independent will forces. They are being carefully enticed to enter more and more deeply into the virtual world created by someone we do not know, whose motivations are not revealed to us.

To the defenseless children who innocently accept everything in the environment as of equal value, screen time predisposes them to look outward for engagement and "feeling good." It distracts them from growing strength inwardly. It predisposes the child to depend on a substance or a behavior that directs and controls him rather than directing himself from his inner place of strength.

So we come back to where we began. The foundation for preventing addiction lies in early childhood. We give our children strength to face perilous future temptations if we give their forces of will meaningful and potent chances to develop. We serve our children by protecting them from technological distractions that rob them of opportunities to be active. The possibility of addiction for any of us is frightening, most especially when we think of our children. We all wish to give them the chance to develop their own self-confidence and competence, so to addictive invitations to "feel good" through something external, they can say, "No, thanks. I do it myself."

Guiding
Childhood's Inner Life

The Fairy Tale Path into Life

Protecting Young Children's Steps

The fairy tale has stood for generations as the picture of the human being entering into life. Often the main character of the story is a simple soul. He embarks upon a journey that leads to complications and challenges. The lad sometimes responds with uncomplicated and generous deeds to protect and help another. For example, the simple brother in "The Queen Bee" protects the ants, bees and ducks his more worldly brothers wish to harm. His brothers ridicule him as unsophisticated and foolish. Their motto is to look out for yourself and take what will benefit you. To care about others is foolish and absurdly naïve. When each of the brothers is given impossible tasks, the worldly brothers fail and are turned to stone. The simple one is assisted by all the creatures he has helped and wins the hand of the princess.

A feminine picture of this compassion and generosity is shown in "The Star Money." The little maiden with no possessions besides her clothes and a crust of bread trusts herself "to the good God" and goes out into the world. She gives away everything she has to others more needful than herself. Then the linen dress and golden coins rain down upon her from the heavens. She has no want for the rest of her days.

A sillier picture of this comes in the English folk tale of "Lazy Jack." Our modern view would see Jack as "not the sharpest knife in the drawer." At his mother's insistence he goes into the world to find work. He has many mishaps because he applies his mother's advice literally to situations that don't match. He carries in his hand the coin he was paid as wages. This he drops and loses in the stream. Mother tells him he should have carried it in his pocket. When he is next paid a jug of milk, he happily pours the liquid into his pocket, with very sticky and unsatisfactory results. So it goes until he appears such a ludicrous fellow, carrying a donkey on his shoulder, that he makes the sad merchant's daughter laugh for the first time in her life. This opens the future for them to marry and live well ever after. In the end, his lack of shrewdness has been his gift, not his disability.

The little child is supposed to be a simpleton, a naïve soul guided by cosmic wisdom that streams in with her through the portal of birth. Experience in the world through time develops into a body of knowledge which helps the child respond more practically and successfully—in the world's eyes—to new situations. But the experience has to come before the concept can arise and guide future deeds in the world.

The world as it confronts little children now wants to "fracture the fairy tale." Pushing abstractions and concepts upon younger and younger minds makes the world a perplexing place. True knowledge comes through experience, observation of that experience, and forming possible conclusions that embrace all one has witnessed. The little child's opened-eyed and non-judgmental path is a foundation for Goethean observation skills. Waldorf early childhood education world-wide is striving to help our unworldly simpletons navigate a fractured world so they can find their way to the riches of life at the end. ✿

Little Children
and Simplicity

*S*implifying is an impulse poking up in mainstream thinking; it is already well considered in Waldorf education circles. Life is sufficiently complicated that adults feel pulled under by the pace of life, level of stimulation, and daily expectations we hold for ourselves. We seem to intuitively know that "less is more." Doing fewer things more thoroughly can be more satisfying than quickly attending to a lot of slivers and fragments of life. What is done consciously and well contributes to the general quality of life for ourselves and others. To simplify, we allow less to distract our attention and consciousness so our focus to what we are doing is more devoted.

Little children are perfect teachers to show what this simple approach means. With spring now awakening, picture a little child in a quiet garden. The child wanders with openness to take in whatever is there and sees a tiny blossom emerging from the brown earth. She will likely squat down and look with devoted attention to the little flower, brush it with finger tips, perhaps pluck it up out of the earth, smell it, look at its shape and color. Next the child may notice a worm or ladybug nearby. Here, too, the little creature is explored through all these sensory avenues. The child spends a sustained time communing with these small, natural expressions of life. In a healthy young child the senses are open to noticing the small things, savoring them, and being satisfied that what she has experienced is enough.

For these faculties to stay alive and grow, protection from the stimulus of daily life is essential. If the human being is bombarded by things coming too fast, too loud, too bright, too big, too many, then two different things may happen. One is that the sensory stimulation is so overwhelming that the person simply shuts off and notices almost nothing. This person withdraws in a kind of shock. Another is that the habituated level of receiving stimulation is so high that only the biggest, brightest, and loudest impression receives any attention; this child may seek stronger and more frequent stimulation because anything less does not register. Everything else more modest and subtle cannot compete in this sensory contest. Then we respond to what is most insistent, not necessarily what is most important. As we look at our harried adult lives, we wonder how to enable our children to create healthy lives for themselves and their future families. Wordsworth said, "The child is father of the man." As the child is protected from the overwhelming hustle and bustle of life, so her natural impulse to be content with less can grow as a habit pattern for life.

Being able to discern what is essential from what is not is a valuable life skill. If we quiet the environment for the child, reducing unnecessary distractions so the child can discover and explore the small and wonderful, we are planting the seed for an adult capacity to discern the essential, which may be something quiet and subtle, not something screaming for attention. As parents and educators of children, we want to protect and encourage this growing capacity. When we protect and simplify for the child's sake, we also reclaim our childhood heritage of looking at the small blossom or ladybug in the grass. Experiencing the simplicity of less-is-more benefits us, too.

Children's Questions—
What Are They Really Asking?

*L*ittle children ask endless questions. The initial wordless finger pointing, which might mean "Take me there," "What is that?" or "I want," eventually gives way to verbalization. The first questions begin to emerge at about 18-24 months and are mostly "What?" But the third year brings more "W" questions: Who? When? Where? and Why? When children are just beginning to question, it is easy for our answers to be guided by their young state of consciousness that is just awakening to the world around them. A simple answer is fully satisfying. "That is a cow. When the cow talks, she says, 'Moo.'" If we have the restraint to stop there, most often the child feels he has an adequate answer and asks no more. He takes in the visual impression and the word and starts to build up his construct of the world, matching the picture of what he has seen in real life with its name. Impressions become memory pictures linked with words. He begins to build the essential foundation which his understanding of the world is built upon.

The little child starts with broad concepts, universal words really. For one child "Dada" meant Daddy, Mommy, Grandma, and Doggie—all the essential beings in life at that time. She gradually began to discriminate one from the other in her own time. She listened and absorbed from the language around her as part of life, not from elaborate explanations.

When more complex questions arise, our modern orientation is eager to start sharing scientific facts and details with little children to give them an intellectual head start in this competitive world. To the question, "Where does the sun go at night?" the temptation is strong to describe the rotation of the earth and the sun and earth as part of the solar system; we might just throw in the moon and its relation to the earth for good measure. All this may be true, but it is very abstract and just words the child cannot relate to actual experience. The child is much more likely asking, "Why is it dark?" She will be satisfied and reassured with, "The sun has shown so brightly all day that he is tired. Now he is going to sleep." This is an answer that resonates with the child's level of experience—getting tired and needing rest. Even the sun, so big and powerful, needs to rest, just like the child does. Picture answers like these are comprehensible because the explanation relates to something the child experiences herself.

We adults tend to over-explain with lots of facts. This comes out of our excitement to share our knowledge and interests with our children. This tendency, however, can also be motivated by the fearfulness that permeates our society. We get anxious that our children will not learn enough fast enough to navigate a satisfying life. The world is racing by us adults so fast that we can hardly keep up with it. Will our children be competent and competitive? We worry about them.

We needn't. The time for scientific facts will come, and the children will be eager for them. In Waldorf education this begins in earnest in the middle school years when facts can be added to a rich, solid foundation built on truthful yet simple, pictorial answers. Too much explanation can be overwhelming. When your child asks a question, try giving a simple answer and then stop. If the child really wants more, he will ask. Many children's questions are asking for reassurance of how something fits into his life, not a factual discourse. If we truly watch and listen, our children will guide us to know what their questions are really asking. ✿

Whose Idea
Is Your Child Thinking?

*I*t is our fondest hope as parents and teachers that our children will be allowed to encounter the world directly through the freshness and unprejudiced vision of their own eyes, ears, and hands. I think of our grandson's dedication to snail-watching last spring and summer. Nothing was more interesting to him. And through his devotion to watching these small creatures, he began to form his own personal image of "snail-ness." Another child has a special attentiveness to sounds—bird song, bug buzz, carefully articulated speech in nursery rhymes that invite her interest in the spoken word. She loves to sing and echoes back the simple, sweet sounds of her mother's voice that have not been digitally engineered. At the very beginning of life, touching (and, of course, tasting) are the avenues for learning about the world. This begins with the warmth of the parent's nestling chest, the sweet taste of milk. Then the child learns so much about the texture and character of different materials—wood with its slivers and splinters, pine cones with their pungent smell and rough surface, the softness of the favorite blanket that one cannot sleep without. These are all first-hand experiences and resonate deeply into the child.

We want these impressions to be good ones. We know that first impressions are often lasting ones. The first time we experience something, we tend to assume that this is what a particular experience is like. How things are portrayed makes a huge impression upon us, especially on young children, who Rudolf Steiner, the founder of Waldorf education, described as "total sense organ[s]." The little child has no filters and no capacity to discriminate, and knows if something is desirable and true or untrue. Children accept all experiences equally. They are quite defenseless.

These simple experiences are available to our children, but it is getting harder and harder to find them in unadulterated or unexaggerated form. Children and adults alike are bombarded with media imaginations of how the originator of the video, toy, song, or advertising piece wants us to view their product. These are usually loud with stylized speech, stereotyped with unrealistic and distorted body parts and facial features, and show exaggerated behavior—louder, faster, and more clever and slick than we know real people to be—and, more importantly, than we want our children to be. These impressions are taken in deeply where they lodge in the child's memory collection of "this is what the world is like."

There are many good reasons to reduce children's screen time and other media exposure. Without the distraction of media, children have richer opportunities for free, creative play; for exploration of the world; for developing social play with others; for developing healthy sensory systems through lots of unstructured movement; for helping with practical life in the home to learn how real people live their lives. Children can experience life actively, rather than passively sitting and taking in someone else's ideas of the world.

As a Waldorf educator I have shared all of these points with families over many years. But recently it has struck me strongly that a most compelling reason to shelter our children from media is to protect them from other people's representations of the world that we know are not true. These impressions are difficult to erase. Waldorf education is all about supporting the development of free and independent thinkers, who have the capacity to chart their own course in the world. Our media-dominated society is working hard to saturate our minds with ideas of how they would like us to think about the world. Speaking personally, I do not want these people, whose motives probably have more to do with profit than the welfare of our children, to form the children's view of the world and human relationships. The next time we consider letting our child see media, please ponder: Whose idea will this cause my child to think? Does it have worth that will guide my child well into life? Will it add to the foundation upon which an upright life can grow?

There are so many things in life we cannot control. Our children's media exposure is something we can.

Gender Identity:
More Complicated Than Ever

_G_ender has been a persistent, complicated topic since the time of Adam and Eve. Masculinity and femininity have been characterized in many ways. Sometimes these categories are stereotypes that trap individuals in gender-role expectations that freeze and paralyze potential and diversity. More objective observations can give us important insight into common inclinations that can come with being born into a female or male body. Yet anthroposophy urges us to go even further. The ultimate goal is to recognize and affirm the personhood beyond gender, the personhood which lies within the innermost core of one's eternal being.

The civil rights and feminist movements of the 1960s and their continued reverberations have enabled us to become more flexible and generous in our feeling and thinking toward human diversity. Thank goodness, for "the times, they are [still] a-changing." Increasing numbers of children are rattling and challenging how we think about the human gender experience. These new messengers of "otherness" are transgender and gender-fluid children. They announce with clarity and conviction that their biological bodies—and consequently the role expectations assigned to them at birth—do not fit with who they experience themselves to be. These children are proclaiming that biology does not dictate gender identity in their cases. And these statements are coming from such young ages that we know their pronouncements arise from some source other than societal influences. How are we to respond to this? How can we understand this? How can we honor this? How does this question relate to Waldorf early childhood and its protective embrace of the young child?

Waldorf early childhood education protects the child from being overwhelmed by the world. Instead of the rush and bustle of erratic schedules and sensory overload, it offers experiences that nourish the senses with beauty, goodness, and truth. Hence we have the aesthetically arranged classrooms with soft colors, quiet voices and songs, and simple playthings made of natural materials. The objective is to protect and nurture the eternal individuality

of each child so it may freely awaken in good time and flower into the unique expression of who that person has come to be, into what gender expression that may be.

It is tempting to assign words such as "quaint," "sweet," and "old-fashioned" to this approach. But these descriptors do not appreciate the historical moment when the impulse for Waldorf education was called into being. The political, social, economic, and cultural life of post-World War I Germany was in shambles. Rudolf Steiner was asked if he had ideas for a new form of education that would give humanity a chance to save itself from devastation. Waldorf education was the response. At that time it was, and it still remains, bold and courageous. It stands boldly as an alternative to the rush toward technological and strict academic education. These current trends claim to prepare children for the uncertainties of the future that make us feel anxious. But such teaching forgets the human being along the way. The unfolding, developing human being stands at the center point of Waldorf education—in whatever form "they" come towards us. It is the fully developed human being who feels capable and valued who has the best preparation to meet future uncertainties, no matter what form they take.

This thought takes us back to these special, gender-jolting children joining our families and school classes. Anthroposophy reminds us to pay attention to "the signs of the times." These children—and their forerunners who are now adults carrying this unique gender experience—are a profound "sign of the times." Young children are said to bring "the latest news from the spiritual world." One message we can clearly read is, "Do not judge me or think you can understand me by what you see. Look and listen below and within the externals to know me." We can come to know who they are and what gifts they bring by holding back assumptions and by being sincerely interested in them. This is an important message to our world where the rhetoric of politics, religion, race, and ethnicity show drastic polarization and intolerance. Understanding and honoring these children is one step in countering the divisive mood of the world.

In being true to our Waldorf mandate to be bold and courageous as well as sheltering, the Waldorf Early Childhood Association (WECAN) has pledged to explore transgender and gender-fluid issues in our journal, *Gateways*. The International Association of Steiner/Waldorf Early Childhood Education council (IASWECE) is launching a study of this human expression as well. These children have been brave enough to come into this complicated world. We need to be equally brave to challenge our own assumptions so we do not let them down. We have much to learn for, about, and from them.

Against Fear:
The Michaelmas Call

We live in a fear-filled world. This has always been true for humanity. Whether it has been threat from wild beasts, natural disasters, famine and starvation, war, plague and illness, or material poverty, humanity has always had big worries. In our own time we experience strongly that fear and anxiety fill the air we breathe every day as well. It is a hard fear-state to deal with because we do not know from where or when a threat may come. This fills us with vague, consistent anxiety. And as parents, we feel fear about our children's safety and the security of their future. We want to protect them and keep them safe. So we should. We want to defend them, reducing the chance that our children will be physically injured, emotionally wounded, or socially challenged. In reasonable proportion, this is all good. We do not want to submit them to experiences that will overwhelm them. What used to be seen as "making children tough" can now be recognized as insensitivity at best or abuse and neglect when extreme. These we know can irreparably damage children. They can become hardened, inclined toward bullying and aggression, or cower in fearful withdrawal.

Yet a stronger temptation of our current times pulls us in an opposite direction. We want to take no chances with our children's safety or happiness and become so protective that we effectively wrap them up in "cotton wool." We can become the classic "helicopter parents" who monitor and control everything we can. This has its problems. Living in a controlled environment with reduced challenges does not help children develop skills for living into an uncertain future.

If we look deeply into what is influencing our decisions, we find our own fearfulness. Coming from Old English, the word "fear" originally meant "sudden attack, ambush, or snare." These are timely images that apply to the mood of our lives now. Our own anxieties magnify our fearfulness about what our children may have to confront. So what are we to do?

So much of current education looks to *skill development and technological training* as "insurance" toward the future. Yet we see that skills become quickly obsolete with the rapid technological advances streaming—maybe even screaming—towards us. So perhaps a more fundamental question is, What are the human *capacities* we can develop to meet the challenges of an uncertain future? The capacity to respond to the unexpected with flexibility and creativity is one. It is healthy to be surprised, even momentarily stunned by a surprise. But we do not become paralyzed in fear. The capacity to take reasonable, healthy risk is another. This means stepping toward a new, unfamiliar experience, even if feeling anxious. We can feel nervous but not paralyzed with fear.

How do we give our children opportunity to develop these capacities? A great insight Rudolf Steiner has shared is that children live into who and what we adults *are* rather than what we say. They absorb our unspoken attitudes and emotions. If we live in fearfulness, this is what our children will experience. They will absorb our reluctance to enter into life, holding ourselves back in protective gestures. This is prudent and healthy at certain times; but if this is our life gesture, one cannot truly and fully live.

The fall festival of Michaelmas is about fear and courage. Archangel Michael fights the dragon. This happens year after year. The dragon is never fully quashed. Michael confronts it again and again, never backing away or giving up. Nothing in the stories say that he is fearless. He confronts fear by looking it squarely in the face and refusing to become paralyzed by it. In subtle ways, over-protectiveness encourages a kind of paralysis. It allows less and less activity and exploration so the gestures of living become more and more narrow. To be responsive to what lies ahead for us in the future, we need to be nimble and adaptable. Living in a cloud of unnamed fearfulness stills and freezes.

If we do not want our children to be narrowed by fear, we must break out of our own fetters. Michaelmas stories of courage are usually told to children. But the challenge is for us adults is to look into our own lives. Where does my fear live within me? How can I look it in the face and find my own boldness to confront that which intimidates me? How can I protect my child but not smother? How can I find my inner certainty in the goodness of life so my child and I can walk forth in the spirit of Michael? 🌿

Other WECAN Books you will enjoy

Tell Me a Story
Stories from the Waldorf Early Childhood Association of North America

Edited by Louise deForest
A collection of over 80 inspiring and nourishing stories from the members and friends of the Waldorf Early Childhood Association

Toy Making:
Simple Playthings to Make for Children
Gun Lee Blue

Basic techniques and instructions for classic playthings to foster creativity and imagination.   **$22**

Play with Us!
Freya Jaffke

Games for indoors and outdoors, building skills and dexterity as well as for the pure joy of play.   **$18**

Let's Dance and Sing!
Freye Jaffke

Songs, verses, games, and dances to give children the joy of singing and playing together. Companion to *Play with Us!*   **$18**

845-362-1690 • info@waldorfearlychildhood.org
store.waldorfearlychildhood.org